To: Hanna
From: Mark & Linda Eigsti
4-17-06

THE STORY OF JESUS

BY EIRA REEVES

Chariot Books™
David C. Cook Publishing Co.

Published by Chariot Books™,
an imprint of
David C. Cook Publishing Co,
Elgin, Illinois 60120

ISBN 0 784 0777 X

Designed by Peter Wyart
Created by Three's Company,
12 Flitcroft Street,
London WC2H 8DJ

Worldwide co-edition organised
and produced by
Angus Hudson Ltd,
Concorde House,
Grenville Place,
London NW7 3SA

Printed in Singapore

CONTENTS

Many, many years ago, Jewish prophets foretold that a special Man would be born in the town of Bethlehem.

They said He would be
called the Prince of Peace.

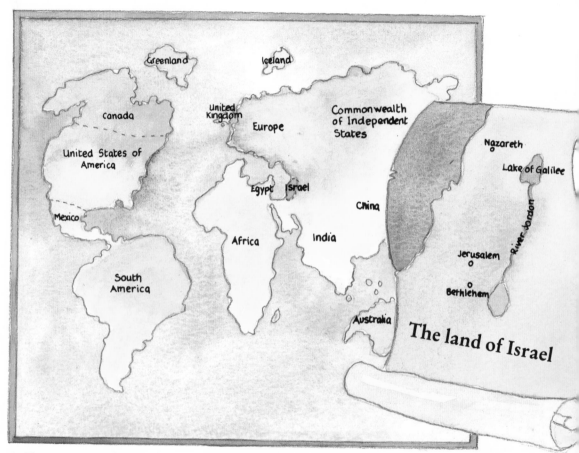

The World

6

The
first Christmas

It all began in a little town called
Nazareth...

In Nazareth there lived a young
woman called Mary.
One day an angel appeared to her.
He said, 'You will give birth to a
very special baby. You must call
the baby Jesus.'

9

Mary went quickly to tell her cousin Elizabeth the good news.
Elizabeth was expecting a baby too.
His name was to be John.
Both women were overjoyed.

Mary was married to a carpenter named Joseph.
They had to go on a long journey to Bethlehem.
Mary was very tired when they arrived.

At first they could find nowhere to sleep

Then a hotelkeeper found them a stable, where the animals were kept. Mary and Joseph took it gladly.

That night some shepherds were sleeping in a field near
Bethlehem. Suddenly they saw a bright light. An angel
appeared and said, 'Tonight a child has been born in
Bethlehem. He has come to save His people.'

14

Immediately the shepherds set off to find the newborn baby.

Far away, some wise men saw a special new star in the sky.
They knew they must follow this star to find a special baby.
So they brought gifts of gold, frankincense and myrrh to
give to the child.

16

The visitors came to the little town of Bethlehem, where the star was shining down.

When they saw the baby Jesus, they bowed down and worshiped Him.

Jesus grows up

Mary and Joseph took Jesus back to their own town, Nazareth.

ere Jesus grew up. He helped His parents
d played with His friends.

When Jesus was twelve, He went with His parents to the city of Jerusalem for the festival called Passover. But Mary and Joseph lost Him in the crowd

At last they found their son again; He was talking to the Jewish teachers in the Temple.
Everyone was amazed at the wise things He said.

As the years passed, Jesus grew up.
He began to work as a carpenter,
like His father Joseph.
He was happy working with His
hammer and saw.
But He knew that God had a very
special job for Him to do.

24

Jesus' special work

At this time Jesus' cousin, John, started to preach
by the river Jordan.
He told people to turn from the bad things they were doing.

He dipped them in the river to
show that they were making a
clean start.

Jesus came to the river and asked John to baptize Him too.

The Holy Spirit came down on Him like a dove.

This was the beginning of Jesus'
special work, the work God
wanted Him to do.

29

Now Jesus went to the lake. He called twelve men to be His special followers. These men were called disciples.

Their names are:
Simon Peter
and his brother
Andrew,
James
and his brother *John,*
Philip,
Bartholomew,
Matthew the tax-man,
Thomas the twin,
another *James,*
Simon,
Judas, James' son,
and *Judas.*

He taught His disciples
how to pray to God, our
heavenly Father:

Our Father in heaven:
Holy is Your name;
May Your kingdom
    come;
May Your will be done
on earth as it is in heaven.
Give us today the food we
    need.
Forgive us the wrong we
    have done,
as we forgive those who
    have wronged us.
Do not bring us to hard
    testing,
but keep us safe from evil.
    Amen.

Jesus began to travel to nearby towns and villages.

He told people special stories about how God wants our world to be. Everyone was amazed when they heard Him speak.

Jesus loved children.
He said that we should love them and take good care of them.

He wanted all people to love
one another.
He told us always to forgive
each other.

Many sick people came to Jesus – people who were crippled,
blind or deaf.

Jesus healed them.

And with His Father's help Jesus did special miracles.
One day He fed five thousand people with just five loaves
and two fish!

Jesus
goes to Jerusalem

Jesus loved Jerusalem, the capital city.
It was very beautiful.

Jesus decided to travel to Jerusalem again.
On the way, He said to His disciples, 'I am going to die soon.'
The disciples were sad. They didn't know why He was
saying such things.

But some of the leaders in Jerusalem hated Jesus.
They thought He wasn't keeping their laws.
So they plotted to kill Him.

Judas, one of the disciples, turned against Jesus.
He made a secret plan with the people who hated Jesus.

When Jesus arrived in Jerusalem it was the time of the
Passover festival again. He asked to borrow a donkey,
because He wanted to ride into the city.

46

When they saw Him coming, people waved palm leaves.
'Jesus is our King!' they shouted.

Later, Jesus had a special feast with His disciples.
He said once more, 'I am going to die soon!'
But they didn't understand why He was saying this.

Jesus tore off some bread and poured some wine. He said,
'Each time you eat bread and drink wine, remember Me.'

Then Jesus and the disciples went out into a garden.
Jesus prayed to His heavenly Father.
But the disciples fell asleep.

The first Easter

While they were in the garden, Judas brought Jesus' enemies
to arrest Him.
Jesus' disciples and friends all ran away.

The soldiers brought Jesus before the Roman ruler, Pilate.
But Pilate could find no fault in Jesus.

When Pilate brought Jesus before
the people, they shouted,
'Kill Him! Kill Him!'

The soldiers took Jesus and put Him to death
on a wooden cross.

Jesus' friends and family were very sad. They had lost a very special friend and leader.

They took Jesus' body, wrapped it carefully in cloth,
and laid it in a cave tomb.
A great round stone was rolled across the door.

57

Two days later Peter and John,
Jesus' disciples, went to visit the tomb.
But the stone had been rolled away.
They were amazed!

58

*Jesus
is alive!*

They saw an angel inside the tomb.
He said, 'Don't be afraid! Jesus is alive!
Go and meet Him in Galilee.'

on afterwards the disciples
ent fishing on the lake of
alilee.

They saw Jesus on the
beach, making a fire.
He invited them to
have breakfast.

Peter was so pleased to see Jesus that he jumped into the water and waded ashore.

In Jerusalem, soon after this, Jesus left them.
He returned to His heavenly Father.
Now the disciples knew He was alive forever.

And Jesus promised to return one day as King ...